How to Make Your Own
UGLY CHRISTMAS SWEATERS

NICOLETTE LAFONSECA

How to Make Your Own
UGLY CHRISTMAS SWEATERS

20 Fun & Easy Holiday Projects to Craft and Create

Racehorse Publishing

First published in Great Britain in 2016 by Quercus Editions Ltd, a Hachette UK company, as *How to Make Your Own Christmas Jumper*.

First Racehorse Publishing Edition 2018.

Racehorse Publishing books may be purchased in bulk at special discounts for sales promotion, corporate gifts, fund-raising, or educational purposes. Special editions can also be created to specifications. For details, contact the Special Sales Department, Skyhorse Publishing, 307 West 36th Street, 11th Floor, New York, NY 10018 or info@skyhorsepublishing.com.

Racehorse Publishing™ is a pending trademark of Skyhorse Publishing, Inc.®, a Delaware corporation.

Visit our website at www.skyhorsepublishing.com.

10 9 8 7 6 5 4 3 2 1

Library of Congress Cataloging-in-Publication Data is available on file.

Print ISBN: 978-1-63158-324-7

Designed and typeset by Rosamund Saunders
Photography by Tiffany Mumford
Stylist: Hannah Read-Baldrey

Printed in China

CONTENTS

INTRODUCTION

Back in the early 2000s, we all laughed as Bridget Jones turned her nose up at Mark Darcy's tasteless reindeer sweater that his mother forced him to wear. We have come a long way since then, and these days he probably wouldn't be the only guest turning up to the party in a novelty knit. In fact, today Bridget would likely be asking why his reindeer sweater did not have any LED lights or sequins on it!

No longer is the Christmas sweater associated only with Bing Crosby at the piano or an embarrassing gift from your granny. Its comeback may have begun as an ironic hipster craze, but the trend has quickly gone mainstream, with a new wave of celebrities in Christmas sweaters flooding our media each year, seen on everyone from pop stars, actors, and TV presenters, to sports stars, politicians, and even rappers!

We humans are a nostalgic bunch—you need only look at the countless retro and vintage products on sale to realize we are in love with the past. There's something comforting about recapturing things the way they were. Even new technology gets dressed up in Grandma's clothes, such as smartphones made to look like eighties cassette tapes, digital cameras that resemble their ancestors, and photo filters that let us transform our sharp modern shots back to the faded snaps of yesteryear. And when it comes to Christmas fashion, the shops are overflowing with sweaters inspired by the ones our elderly relatives used to knit for us, with some retailers reporting festive sweater sales as their financial savior and others stocking over thirty different styles. We would have been pretty grumpy back then when forced to pull on a homemade monstrosity on Christmas morning, but these days we're positively leaping into our Christmas gear, ready to show it off with pride.

Even academics have been trying to get to the bottom of this growing trend. Dr. Matt Slater of Staffordshire University believes it boosts our social identity, since "wearing Christmas [sweaters] helps us feel part of a group and achieve a sense of togetherness that people associate with this time of year." As he points out:

"It's a trend that's very much about socializing, with numerous charity events and tongue-in-cheek [sweater] parties taking place in homes, schools, and offices on both sides of the Atlantic. Whether you wear yours as an ironic statement, a nostalgic homage to days gone by, or to raise money for charity, there's no doubt that Christmas [sweaters] are once more a fixture in our festivities."

But with the trend rocketing, it is increasingly hard to be different. These days, the only route to a truly unique creation is to avoid buying off the peg like everybody else and instead to create your own. And, indeed, there is nothing more rewarding than being able to say, "I made it myself."

But what if you cannot knit? What if your kids announce at the very last minute that they all need Christmas sweaters for a school event? What about the competitive office Christmas sweater party? Whether you fall into one of these categories or, like me, are just crazy for all things Christmas, this is the book for you.

The projects in this book can be tackled by pretty much anyone with opposable thumbs.

It's not about knitting an entire sweater from scratch; it's about clever customizing; taking a plain sweater as your starting point and then having fun making it festive. Each project comes with simple step-by-step instructions, along with photos to inspire you and show what you're aiming for, as well as templates at the back of the book that can be enlarged or reduced to the desired size. The glossary on pages 98–110 will help you learn some essential stitches and other skills that come in handy throughout the rest of the book.

And if you're not a fan of the "ugly" sweater, then fear not: the projects all fall into one of three categories: simply delightful, too cute, or delightfully tacky. If you're feeling really creative, remember you can always crank things up a notch or combine ideas from more than one project, such as matching the snowflakes on page 38 with the LED lights on page 53. And to illustrate that any sweater can be given the Christmas treatment, the photographs show a wide variety of styles, from fluffy sweaters and chunky knits, to polo necks, tunics, and even dog sweaters! With this book to guide and inspire you, you can be pretty certain no one will turn up to the party wearing the exact same outfit as you! Merry Christmas!

GATHERING SUPPLIES

Although each project in this book lists the specific materials you will need, there are plenty of crafty items and festive embellishments you can start to collect that are bound to come in handy. Get those Christmas decorations out of storage, as old tinsel, mini ornaments, shiny beads, and even old Christmas cards can be given a new life as sweater decor. And if you're really organized, you can buy decorations at reduced prices in January to save for the following year.

When it comes to fabrics, if you want to save your pennies, rummage around the house for scraps of material or ruined clothes that can be cut up and repurposed—even old socks can be used, while your local haberdashery store may have a "bargain bin" full of cut-price fabric offcuts.

From November onwards, haberdashery takes on a new life and I defy you not to be in awe of how many glittery ribbons, bows, and knick-knacks you will find there. Look for cute Christmas-themed buttons, appliqués, jingle bells, or shiny fabric—and remember that "shiny" is the cornerstone of any good Christmas sweater! And don't limit yourself by only looking at things that are intended to adorn clothes; the interiors section is also a great place to find decorative braid, lengths of beaded ribbon, fringing or tassels, all of which can be used for the projects in this book.

If you or any of your friends are knitters, save leftover yarn for creating tiny pompoms and miniature bobble hats (see pages 110 and 57). And finally, for the ultimate inspiration, look online. Besides dedicated craft retailers, sites like Amazon, eBay, and Etsy have all manner of festive materials for sale, in every color, shape, and design you could dream of.

MATERIALS

EMBROIDERY FLOSS
Several projects in this book use embroidery floss. It comes in every color and shade imaginable and is sold in skeins. Each length is made up of six finer threads twisted together. In the "Don't Get Cross" sweater (see page 73), which involves a cross-stitch design, the embroidery floss can be used in the thickness it's sold in, for more substantial stitches. In other projects it's better to separate the embroidery floss strands into thirds, using a two-thread thickness for any sewing.

SCISSORS
I suggest investing in a really good pair of fabric scissors that you never use to cut paper or they will dull very quickly. You will also need a regular pair of scissors to use for cutting out paper templates and a small, sharp pair of scissors to cut out fine detail.

SEWING MACHINE
Only one project in this book relies on a sewing machine ("It's S'no Globe," page 45), although much of the other sewing can be done by machine if that's how you prefer to work. Your machine need only have a basic stitch function. Basic sewing machines are available these days for as little as $65 and, believe me, once you have one, you will use it, as they are invaluable for speeding up projects. If you don't have access to a sewing machine, you can complete all the projects (apart from the snow globe) by hand. It will just take a little longer.

NEEDLES AND THREADS
It is useful to have a range of different needles and threads, including a needle with a large eye to accommodate embroidery floss as well as regular thread. A mix of cotton and synthetic threads are useful, in a wide selection of colors, but avoid budget threads and opt for more expensive branded varieties. Cheaper options are a false economy as they break easily and, when using a machine, can cause changes in tension or pulling in your work.

YARN NEEDLE
To finish off yarn projects you will need a yarn needle, sometimes called a darning needle. This has a very large eye and a blunt tip. A plastic one is less likely to catch and pull on the yarn.

CARING FOR YOUR SWEATER

Once you have spent time making a one-of-a-kind Christmas sweater, it's likely you will want to be able to wash it without ruining it. All but two of the designs in this book can be washed—those two are designed as "temporary" sweaters where the fixtures can be easily removed and the sweater returned to normal. You can then wash the sweater as usual and replace the embellishments if you wish. Those sweaters with permanent designs can be placed into a pillowcase, secured with a tight knot at the top so that it cannot open during the cycle, and washed in your machine on the gentle/hand wash setting. Even if the sweater being washed is made of acrylic or mixed fibers and would usually wash on a normal setting, the alterations and embellishments you have added require you to wash it on the gentlest setting.

Gift of the Magi

WHAT BETTER PRESENT TO GIVE TO A LOVED ONE THAN YOUR UNDIVIDED ATTENTION? WITH ITS CHEERY FESTIVE BOW, THIS SWEATER TURNS YOU INTO THE GIFT.

In the midst of the Christmas season, when life is busier than ever, crammed full of visiting, shopping, wrapping, preparing, cooking, and celebrating, it's easy to forget that the people closest to us often want little more than our time. Perhaps set aside a day to spend completely with loved ones, doing all the things they want to do, whether that's watching Christmas movies, playing board games, or going for a wintry walk—all while wearing your festive sweater, of course!

Materials

- 3 generous lengths of wide satin ribbon
- Dress pins
- Needle or sewing machine
- Thread (in a coordinating color to ribbon)
- Scissors

Method

1 Lay your sweater flat on a surface you can work on comfortably.

2 Place your first length of ribbon vertically down the front of the sweater, so that it runs down the center from neck to hem. Pin in place, allowing about ⅛ inch of extra ribbon at top and bottom (this will later get turned under for a neat edge). Cut off any excess neatly.

3 Using a needle and coordinating thread, attach the ribbon to the sweater using a straight running stitch (see glossary, page 109). Alternatively, you can pin the ribbon in position and then stitch it down with a sewing machine if you prefer. Turn both ends of the ribbon under before sewing them down, folding back the excess ⅛ inch that you kept for this purpose, so that the raw edges are hidden underneath.

4 Lay a second length of ribbon horizontally across the front of the sweater, through the middle from left to right, and overlapping the first ribbon to form a cross. Pin in place, cut off any excess neatly (again leaving ⅛ inch extra at both ends), and stitch down by hand or by machine, folding the raw ends under as before.

5 Tie the final length of ribbon into a lavish bow. Place this in the center of the sweater at the point where the two other ribbons cross.

6 Attach the bow to the sweater by stitching into the central "knot," starting from the inside of the sweater and bringing the needle out through the fabric and up through all the layers of ribbon, apart from the very top layer of the knot so that the stitch remains invisible. Then push it back down again through all the layers. Repeat the same stitch several times to ensure the bow is well secured. Knot and trim the thread on the inside of the sweater.

7 Make sure the two loose ends of the bow are cut sharply and neatly with fabric scissors. Add a few tiny individual stitches to hold the loops and tails of the bow in position and prevent them drooping or flapping around. Remove all pins from the sweater before wear.

We All Want Some Figgy Pudding

ALTHOUGH FIGGY PUDDING EARNS ITS PLACE IN THE SONG "WE WISH YOU A MERRY CHRISTMAS," YOU MIGHT BE SURPRISED TO DISCOVER IT IS NOT THE SAME THING AS CHRISTMAS PUDDING.

It is, in fact, paler and typically contains figs (the clue is in the name!). But since it features in a Christmas carol, it is arguably just as festive. Depending on how dark brown your sweater is, you can choose which pudding you'd rather call it after. The most important thing here is that the garment you use is brown in color. A rounded neckline is also recommended. The white collar represents the brandy sauce poured over the top of your pudding and the holly "crown" adds a fun decorative touch. If you don't want your holly on a headband, you could instead affix it to a dark-colored hat or cap. This is one pudding I definitely don't advise setting light to!

Materials

- Small black felt balls/mini pompoms (as many as you like)
- Needle and coordinating threads
- White felt, fabric, or lace
- Plastic-headed pins
- Scissors

Method

1. Decide how many felt balls you want to attach to your sweater. These represent the "figs" or dried fruit in your pudding, so if you like yours particularly fruity, you might wish to increase the pompoms accordingly.

2. With a coordinating thread, sew the balls onto the front of the sweater, attaching each ball with 2–3 stitches before tying off and trimming on the inside of the fabric to secure. You can also add balls to the back if you want.

3. Once you are happy with the number of "figs" you have added, it is time to top your pudding with "brandy sauce." The sweater in the photograph is topped with white felt, but you might alternatively decide to use a white chiffon scarf, lace, or other fabric.

4. With scissors, cut out the white felt or fabric to fit around the top of your sweater, giving it a curved top edge to follow the rounded shape of the neckline, and a wavy bottom edge to resemble drips. Cut out a similar piece to fit around the back.

5. Pin the white collar at intervals around the neckline of your sweater.

6. Once the collar is pinned in position, stitch both pieces down along the top edge using white thread and a straight running stitch (see glossary, page 109), knotting and trimming on the inside of the sweater to secure. The wavy bottom edges can be left loose. Remove the pins before wear.

Holly Crown

Materials

- Paper "holly" template (see page 87)
- Green felt
- Scissors
- Fabric glue
- A plain headband
- Red felt balls/mini pompoms

1. Use the template to cut out 15–20 holly leaves from green felt.

2. Glue leaves lengthways along the top of the headband using fabric glue, overlapping them so that none of the band shows through. Glue three further leaves to the top, arranging them like a little holly sprig (as shown in the photograph), positioned slightly to one side of the band.

3. Once the top of your headband is covered and your sprig is in place, glue more of the leaves to the underside of the headband to neaten the whole thing up and make it more secure. Leave to dry.

4. Once the glue has fully dried, add two or three red felt balls to the center of the sprig, gluing them at the point where the three leaves meet, to resemble a cluster of holly berries. Again leave to dry.

5. Your holly crown is ready to be popped onto your head as a festive finishing touch to your "pudding."

Fill Your Stocking

HAVE YOUR CHRISTMAS STOCKING AND WEAR IT, TOO! A PERFECT WAY TO RECYCLE KIDS' SOCKS, WHICH CAN BE STUFFED WITH SWEETS, TOYS, OR GIFTS TO MAKE FRIENDS SMILE.

Remember that feeling of going to bed on Christmas Eve, so excited you couldn't even begin to imagine sleeping? Eventually you drift off, and the next time you open your eyes you do so tentatively. Is it Christmas yet? A glance at your stocking confirms matters. Strange shapes and bulges protrude from all over it. SANTA HAS BEEN HERE!

The beauty of a Christmas stocking is that you can fill it with anything and those items instantly become fantastic because they were found in a stocking (satsumas, walnuts, coal!). The same goes for these mini stockings, which are made from cute baby socks for extra smiles. Any type of sweater can be used here.

Materials

- Ribbon, embroidery floss, or decorative cord
- Needle and coordinating thread
- Baby socks (raid the dollar store!)
- Decorative mini pegs and bows
- Selection of sweets, candy canes, and/or small toys

Method

1. Lay your sweater flat on a work surface and determine the placement of your ribbon or embroidery floss so that it looks like it is "strung" from one side of the sweater to the other, as if festooned across the front of an invisible mantelpiece.

2. Stitch down your ribbon or floss at both ends, leaving it to hang loose in between or, if you prefer things fixed in a specific position, you can stitch it down along the length using a straight running stitch (see glossary, page 109) or with small individual stitches at intervals.

3. Space your mini socks equally across the front of the sweater, positioning them at an angle with one top "corner" of each sock touching the ribbon garland, as shown, so that they appear to be hanging from a mantelpiece.

4. Attach the socks to the sweater using a needle and coordinating thread, sewing around the outer edge of each one with a straight running stitch (see glossary, page 109), starting at the top corner and catching the ribbon in the first stitch. Remember to leave all the socks open at the top so that they can be filled. Alternatively, if you're in a hurry, you can attach each sock just by its top two corners, securing with individual stitches and leaving the heel and toe hanging loose.

5. Decorate the stockings and ribbon garland as you wish. The sweater in the main photograph is embellished with mini metallic pegs at the top of each stocking and decorative bows stitched onto either end of the garland.

6. For a fun finishing touch, stuff the socks with sweets, candy canes, small toys, or other festive goodies. You're bound to be the most popular guest at the Christmas party when you start doling out the treats!

Let's Make a Snowman!

IF YOU'VE EVER BUILT A SNOWMAN, YOU HAVE PARTICIPATED IN ONE OF THE OLDEST FORMS OF FOLK ART. THE EARLIEST-KNOWN SNOWMAN ILLUSTRATION DATES FROM 1380!

Centuries later, we still rush out as soon as flakes begin to fall, and yet building a snowman remains surprisingly tricky, often resulting in little more than a sad grey pile of sludge topped with a soggy hat. The problem, apparently, is that your snow must be exactly at melting point. If you're lumbered with the "wrong" type of snow—or indeed no snow at all!—what's vastly easier to find is yarn. It needn't be expensive, any ball of cheap acrylic works fine here. The finished snowman is heavy so choose a sweater that can take its weight without becoming misshapen. Customize your new pal with a colorful scarf, cosy hat, or even jingle bell buttons, safe in the knowledge that he won't suddenly melt into an oversized puddle.

Materials

- Sturdy cardboard
- Pencil and ruler
- Scissors
- 2 x 1-lb balls of acrylic white yarn
- Yarn needle
- Paper "arm" templates (see page 87)
- Scraps of brown, black, white, orange, and green felt
- Fabric marker pen
- Fabric glue (optional)
- Needle and coordinating threads
- Two buttons

Method

1. Begin by referring to the "Pompoms" instructions in the glossary section, page 110. Cut the cardboard for the pompoms into rectangles of the following sizes (or adjust as necessary to fit your chosen sweater): small (4 inch), medium (6 inch) and large (8 inch).

2. Once you have made all three pompoms and trimmed them neatly, lay your sweater on a flat surface and determine the placement of the pompoms on the front of the garment.

3. Attach the smallest pompom (head) and largest pompom (base of body) only, leaving a gap in the middle for the medium-sized pompom. To attach, use the long tails that you left for this purpose. Thread one of the tails onto the yarn needle and pull the yarn through the sweater. Working on the inside of the sweater, weave the end through the back of the sweater's stitches until you run out of yarn. Repeat with the second tail. To prevent the pompoms falling forward when the sweater is worn, fix firmly in place using the same process as you did with the tails; take strands from the back of the pompom (the part next to the sweater) and pull them through and secure.

4. Trace the arm templates from page 87, or resize on a photocopier if required. Cut out with scissors.

5. Draw around the arm templates onto brown felt using fabric marker, then cut out using scissors. The arms will be attached to the sweater pen-side down so don't worry if parts of the outline still show.

6　Place the arms on the sweater so that the "shoulder" part of each arm will be covered by the final middle pompom, once it's attached. Fix the arms in place using a little fabric glue, or sew into position using brown thread and a straight running stitch (see glossary, page 109).

7　Now use the same method as before to attach the medium pompom into place.

8　To make the "carrot" nose, cut a square of orange felt and roll into a cone shape. With a needle and orange thread, sew a few tiny stitches to secure the cone shape and prevent it from unrolling. To attach, bring the needle though the sweater from the inside, coming out through the smallest pompom and then sewing into the base of the felt cone. Take the needle back through all the layers to complete the stitch. Two or three repetitions should be enough to secure the nose in place on the front of the upper pompom. Knot and trim the thread on the inside of the sweater.

9　For the eyes, cut two circles of black felt and two slightly smaller circles of white felt. Glue or stitch a white circle onto the front of each black circle. Attach both eyes to the snowman's head in the same way that you attached the nose, tying off securely inside the sweater.

10　To finish, glue or stitch two buttons to the middle pompom, and cut out a green felt scarf that can also be glued or stitched into place.

You Know Dasher and Dancer ...

CHRISTMAS IS THE ONE TIME OF YEAR WHEN YOU CAN GET AWAY WITH BEING KITSCH, TACKY, AND DOWNRIGHT SILLY! SO WHY NOT EMBRACE IT? THIS SWEATER CERTAINLY DOES.

When it comes to Christmas, forget being classy. Who wants a restrained color palette on their tree? I believe the more twinkly lights and sparkly nonsense the better. If you're with me on this, and agree that knitting your own sophisticated Fair Isle sweater in expensive yarn is completely missing the point, then this kitsch and colorful reindeer design is for you. It's a quick project that kids will love and can be customized using any other festive stuffed toy that you can lay your hands on. You're best choosing a robust full-knit sweater here, since delicate fine-knit or lacy open-weave fabrics won't hold the weight of the stuffed toy.

Materials

- A stuffed reindeer toy or any brown teddy
- Baby vest or T-shirt (optional)
- Scissors
- Needle and coordinating threads
- "Tail" template (see page 88)
- Craft stuffing (optional)

Method

1. Cut off the head, arms, and legs of your teddy (if you have children you may need them to leave the room at this point, or there will probably be tears!). Don't throw away the torso as you will need it later.

2. Position the baby vest or T-shirt roughly in the center of the sweater. Pad with craft stuffing for a fuller-figured look! Place the head, arms, and legs of the toy around the baby clothing, making sure the cut ends are concealed and tucked under the baby vest.

3. Once you are happy with their placement, sew everything securely into place using coordinating threads and blind ladder stitch (see glossary, page 100).

4. Use the template on page 88 to make a tail using leftover fur from the torso. Stuff with the leftover filling and secure to the rear of the sweater using blind ladder stitch as before.

Reindeer Antlers

- Paper "antler" template (see page 88)
- Light-brown felt
- Fabric marker pen
- Needle and coordinating thread
- Glue gun
- Fabric glue

1. Trace the template on page 88, or enlarge as desired using a photocopier, and cut out. Draw around the template onto light-brown felt with fabric marker, to create four antler shapes. Cut these out.

2. Stitch the felt pieces together in pairs, using running stitch, leaving them open at the bottom.

3. Attach the antlers to the teddy by stitching onto the bear, using blanket stitch (or a safety pin if you are in a hurry!)

4. Wear your sweater with pride!

 **Tip**

If you're really pushed for time, can't find a suitable baby vest, or are making a very small kids' sweater, a speedy "cheat" method is to simply attach the whole toy to the front of the sweater without cutting it into pieces. This is best with a fairly sturdy sweater and a toy that is not too big or heavy.

Elf Yourself

TRANSFORM YOURSELF INTO SANTA'S LITTLE HELPER IN THIS MOST ICONIC OF CHRISTMAS OUTFITS. SILLY TIGHTS AND HAT ARE ENTIRELY OPTIONAL (GO ON!).

This fun and easy project is bound to get you in the Christmas spirit. You could really go to town and host a Christmas movie marathon, inviting all your friends over to make their own sweaters and drink eggnog before settling down for some festive entertainment, in the form of *Home Alone*, *The Grinch*, and—of course—*Elf*! You do need a green sweater here, though almost any shade will work. It's extremely easy to customize, with buttons, collar, and a belt cut from felt or fabric and attached using a basic straight running stitch. This suits any age or gender—you could even make one for your dog!

Materials

- Paper "elf collar" and "buckle" templates (see page 89)
- Scissors
- Fabric marker pen
- Black and white felt
- Yellow felt or gold metallic fabric
- Dress pins
- Needle and coordinating threads

Method

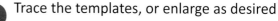

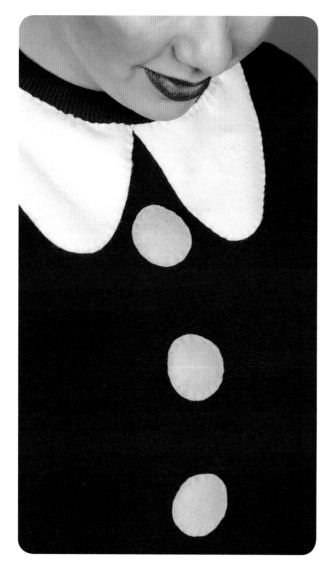

1. Trace the templates, or enlarge as desired using a photocopier, depending on the size of your chosen sweater. Cut them out.

2. Draw around the templates onto the felt with fabric marker, using white felt for the collar, black felt for the belt, and yellow felt or gold fabric for the buckle.

3. Cut out the felt pieces and pin them to the front of your sweater in the positions shown in the photo.

4. Using a needle and coordinating threads, attach the collar and belt pieces to the sweater using a straight running stitch (see glossary, page 109). Knot and trim the threads on the inside of the sweater. Remove all the pins.

5. Cut four small circles from the yellow felt or gold fabric and sew these down the center line of your sweater, with three above the belt and one below. Trim all threads and get ready to elf yourself!

All in the Trimming

WHO NEEDS JEWELRY WHEN YOU CAN DECK YOURSELF IN ORNAMENTS?
WHY STOP AT DECORATING THE CHRISTMAS TREE?

Christmas decorations come in all shapes and sizes, but my favorites are big colorful globes that glimmer and glisten mesmerizingly as they catch the light. Adorned with homemade metallic ornaments, this sweater is a great "temporary" project that can be returned to its original self once Christmas is over. It works best on a loose-knit garment as you will need to push fine ribbon through the weave without making holes in the fabric.

It isn't washable with the ornaments attached, but they can be easily removed and reattached, or used as decorations around your home. Making the ornaments is a fun messy project that children can help with. If you don't have children, you get to have all the fun yourself.

Materials

- Paper "ornament" templates (see page 90)
- Metallic Sharpies or marker pens
- Acetate sheets
- Scissors
- Hole punch
- PVA glue
- Glitter
- Fine ribbon
- Knitting needle or skewer (optional)

Method

 Using the ornament templates on page 90 (or draw your own if you prefer), trace over the shapes and designs onto the acetate sheets in metallic ink. Trace as many ornaments as you wish and then cut them all out from the acetate using scissors.

2. Make a hole at the top of each ornament with the hole punch.

3. Pick out the highlights and patterns of each design by applying PVA glue to those areas and then sprinkling with glitter. Allow to dry for a couple of hours, before dusting off the excess glitter. Repeat this process as necessary.

4. After the final coat of glitter has been applied, cover with another thin layer of PVA glue to seal and leave overnight to dry.

5. Once the top layer is completely dry, use the metallic Sharpies to draw further patterns onto your ornaments in a variety of designs and colors.

6. Cut lengths of fine ribbon and thread one piece through the hole in each ornament. Use this to tie the ornaments onto your sweater, in any pattern or design that you like, pushing the ribbon through the weave with your fingers or with the help of a knitting needle or skewer. Secure each length of ribbon with a neat little bow.

Let it Snow

FOR SOME, SNOW MAKES EVERYTHING APPEAR MORE BEAUTIFUL AND TRANQUIL. FOR OTHERS, IT TURNS THE WORLD INTO A GIANT PLAYGROUND.

Whichever type you are, it's easy to forget that the blanket of white is in fact made up of intricate individual flakes. Next time it snows, sit at the window and watch as flakes hit the pane. If you're lucky, you'll get a split-second glimpse at each stunning design before it melts on the glass, lost forever. This sweater is a tribute to melted snowflakes everywhere. Although the designs may look elaborate, the technique itself is not, since it uses just one very easy type of stitch. You can choose any type of sweater for this project but the white flakes stand out best against a dark color.

Materials

- Yarn needle
- White yarn
- Scissors
- Pompom trim (optional)
- Needle and coordinating thread (optional)

Method

Thread the yarn needle with a generous length of white yarn. (A good rule when hand-sewing is never to thread a length longer than your arm; this helps prevent tangles.)

Using fly stitch (see glossary, page 105), create each frond of your snowflake. It's best to begin with the central vertical frond, which forms the top and bottom of the snowflake. Once these are in place, it is easier to determine the placement of the surrounding fronds. Work from the outside of each frond towards the center.

Play with the length and design of your stitches to make each snowflake design unique.

If you decide to add a pompom trim, attach it to the neckline, cuffs, and bottom of the sweater using coordinating thread and a straight running stitch (see glossary, page 109).

Oh Christmas Tree, Oh Christmas Tree

DECORATING THE CHRISTMAS TREE IS ONE OF THE MOST FUN AND CREATIVE FESTIVE ACTIVITIES. NOW YOU CAN REDECORATE YOURS AS MANY TIMES AS YOU FANCY.

With its detachable decorations, stored in a handy pocket at the base, this sweater lets you change your look whenever the mood takes you, by swapping and rotating your chosen ornaments. Countless different embellishments and materials can be used as tree ornaments, so feel free to think beyond the ideas listed here. Visit a haberdashery and you're bound to be inspired. It's best to choose a thick or sturdy knit for this project, something robust enough to hold all the decorative elements without losing its shape. Use the tree template on page 91 and enlarge to A4 paper or even larger if you like, unless you're an artistic soul who prefers to draw your tree freehand.

Materials

- Paper "tree" template (see page 91)
- Scissors
- Fabric marker pen
- Brown and green felt
- Festive fabric
- Sequin ribbon
- Needle and coordinating threads
- Festive buttons
- Sew-on gems or crystals
- Sew-on Velcro
- Iron-on fabric appliqués in a variety of Christmas designs
- Fabric glue

Method

1. Enlarge the "tree" template on page 91 using a photocopier. Resize as required (you may prefer to make multiple smaller trees rather then one large one), bearing in mind that reducing the size too much can make the tree/s difficult to decorate.

2. Cut the paper template into three sections: pot, trunk, and foliage.

3. Draw around the templates using fabric marker, onto brown felt for the trunk, festive fabric for the pot, and green felt for the foliage section. Make sure to cut the pot on the fold (as shown on template, page 91) for a neat edge, as the top of the pot won't be stitched down, but will be left open for storing spare decorations.

4. It's easiest to add "tinsel" and any fixed ornaments or gems to the foliage section before you attach the tree to the sweater. Arrange the sequin ribbon across your green felt in a zig-zag pattern to resemble tinsel. This looks best with some movement to it, so only stitch it down at the point of each branch and at one or two spots in-between, letting the rest hang freely. To stitch, bring the needle and thread up through the back of the felt and through the center hole in one of the sequins, then back down over the edge of the same sequin and back through the felt, trapping the sequin under the stitch. Go over each stitch several times until it feels secure.

5. Now add "ornaments," in the form of buttons, crystals or whatever sew-on items you've chosen for this purpose. Add these to the tree anywhere you like, apart from the branch points, being as understated or over-the-top as you wish, just like decorating a real tree. Stitch each item down using the method in step 4, taking the thread up through the buttonholes, down over the outside edge and back through the felt, or through whatever hole or loop is available.

6. With tinsel and permanent decorations in place, you can now attach the tree to the sweater and all your stitching on the back will be hidden away. Determine the placement of the tree on your sweater and stitch down the component parts using straight running stitch (see glossary, page 109) and coordinating

threads, starting with the tree trunk, then covering one end of it with the pot and the other end with the foliage.

7 Fold the three cut edges of the pot under and press them with a hot iron. Then stitch down neatly. The top edge will already be neatly turned under as you cut it on the fold of the fabric, so there is no need to iron this. Leave the top of the pot open, ready to be filled with the Christmas appliqués or embellishments you will use as interchangeable decorations.

8 Cut your sew-on Velcro into small squares commensurate to the size of your iron-on appliqués. You will see that the Velcro has two different surfaces—a rigid looped side (the "male" part), and a softer fluffy side (the "female" part). You need to stitch a "male" square to each of the points on the tree. There is a thin line either side of the looping that is softer, where a needle can be pushed through. Attach these patches using straight running stitch (page 109).

9 Glue a "female" Velcro square to the back of each fabric appliqué. Although you are gluing this side you still need to use sew-on Velcro rather than the stick-on kind, as the latter is impossible to stitch through and you'll want your decorations to be well secured to the sweater. The idea is to prepare more appliqué decorations than your tree has space for. (You'll be left with spare "male" parts of Velcro; just discard these).

10 Finally, attach appliqués to each tree point using the Velcro, and store the rest in the pot, ready to be swapped and rotated whenever you fancy a new look.

It's S'no Globe

A SNOW GLOBE IS A MAGICAL AND EXQUISITE ITEM, BELIEVED TO HAVE ORIGINATED IN NINETEENTH-CENTURY FRANCE, AND TREASURED EVER SINCE.

Considered collectibles, snow globes are now sold in tourist destinations all over the world. Gently turn the glass dome and watch as glittery snow swirls and whirls above whatever miniature scene is depicted within. This sweater turns you into a human snow globe, and gives you permission to engage in all manner of funny and ridiculous movements in order to get your "snow" swirling. You might get a few strange looks, but it wouldn't be Christmas without a silly activity, would it? This is the only project in the book that is best done with a sewing machine, since it is involves sewing through plastic, which isn't easily done by hand. However, the stitching technique is pretty straightforward.

Materials

- Paper "globe" templates (see page 92)
- Scissors
- Felt or other non-fraying fabric, in two colors
- Fabric marker pen
- Sewing machine with darning foot
- A4 plastic craft sheet
- Selection of Christmassy fillings (iron-on festive appliqués, beads, small bells, foil party sprinkles, etc.)
- Bean-bag filling
- Glitter
- Dress pins

Method

1. Iron on large pre-bought Christmas appliqués centrally to the sweater.

2. Using an A4 plastic craft sheet and the snow globe template (see page 92) cut out the snow globe pattern to the outside edge.

3. Take the felt and cut out both the outside circle of the snow globe pattern and the base.

4. To combine the elements, firstly place a handful of bean-bag filling and extra stars or glitter on top of the appliqué.

5. Lay the plastic sheet over the top, followed by the round felt edge of the globe and, finally, the base, ensuring that it covers the plastic sheet. Pin into place.

6. Put the darning foot onto your sewing machine. Drop the feed-dog down (these are the teeth that guide your fabric). Every machine will have a slightly different method of doing this, so refer to your manual.

7. On a straight stitch, sew around the outsides of the felt, close to the edge.

Prancing Around

IN HOMAGE TO THE MOST MAGICAL AND MAJESTIC OF CREATURES, THIS TASTEFUL NUMBER WILL KEEP YOU LOOKING CLASSY FOR THE ENTIRE WINTER SEASON.

Understated but attractive, this is a simple project that won't break the bank and involves basic stitching that's easy enough for beginners. You can decorate your sweater with several small reindeer as shown, or alternatively with one large one, or whatever combination you wish. It will work on most types of sweater apart from anything loose-weave or lacy. A sweatshirt is ideal. It would also look good on a patterned sweater with all the reindeer cut from a single contrasting color. The choice is yours.

Materials

- Paper "reindeer" template (see page 93)
- Scissors
- Selection of colored felt
- Iron-on adhesive web
- Iron and ironing board
- Pen or marker
- Needle and coordinating threads
- Small buttons (optional)
- Fabric glue (optional)

Method

1. Enlarge the reindeer template on page 93 to the desired size with a photocopier and cut them out.

2. Lay your felt right-side down and lay the Bondaweb onto the reverse side of the fabric, with the paper side up. (Bondaweb is a fine, paper-backed mesh that becomes adhesive when heat-activated.) You have essentially created a sandwich of felt, Bondaweb and backing paper.

3. Without steam, press a hot iron onto the paper backing of the Bondaweb, making sure you move smoothly over the entire paper.

4. Trace around the reindeer template onto the backing paper of the "sandwich" you have just created. Repeat steps 2–4 to make your desired number of reindeer.

5. Cut out all your reindeer and then gently peel off the backing paper from each one. (Don't throw away the felt-sandwich offcuts.) Place the reindeer shapes onto your sweater, with the Bondaweb side facing down. Make sure you are happy with the placement because as soon as you iron them down, that is where they will stay!

6. Iron each reindeer in place.

7. Finally, to give your reindeer scarves, cut three small rectangles of contrasting felt from the reserved "sandwiched" offcuts. Peel off the Bondaweb backing paper, place each scarf in position, and press with a hot iron. Embellish each with a small button, stitched on or secured with fabric glue. Allow to dry before wear.

Detachable Reindeer Collar

A SIMPLE, CLASSY PROJECT THAT WON'T BREAK THE BANK

Materials

- Paper "collar" and "reindeer" templates (see pages 94 and 93)
- Scissors
- Dress pins
- Soft decorative fabric in color of choice (for front of collar)
- Fabric marker pen
- Sturdy cotton (for back of collar)
- Colored felt (for the reindeer)
- Bondaweb
- Needle and coordinating threads
- Press-stud or hook-and-eye fastening
- Small decorative button (optional)

1 Enlarge the "collar" template on page 94 using a photocopier, and cut out. Pin the paper template to the soft fabric you've chosen for the visible front part of your collar. Trace around the template and cut out the piece of fabric with scissors.

2 Using the template again, cut a second collar shape from some sturdy cotton. (This will act as the underside of your collar so any old pillowcase will do, or some quilting cotton).

3 Trace and cut out two reindeer templates (see page 93) and pin them to the colored felt. Draw around the templates with fabric marker, then cut each shape out with scissors. Attach them to the front part of the collar using the Bondaweb, following the method described for embellishing the sweater. Ensure the right side of the decorative collar fabric is facing up.

4 Secure the reindeer around the edge with straight running stitch (see glossary, page 109) in a matching or contrasting thread.

5 Sandwich the two pieces of collar fabric together with both their "right" sides facing in (i.e. the sides you want to ultimately show). Pin to secure.

6 Use a ¼-inch seam allowance stitch around the collar, leaving a gap of about 2 inches that you will use to turn your collar back around the correct way. Turn out the fabric, easing it out through the hole and pushing into the corners carefully for a neat finish. Close up the gap using a blind ladder stitch (see glossary, page 100).

7 To finish, attach a small press-stud or hook-and-eye to close your collar at the front. Add a small decorative button above the fastening, if you like.

Dreaming of a White Christmas

EVEN THE 'BAH HUMBUG' BRIGADE CAN'T DENY THAT SNOW LOOKS PRETTY. IT MAKES EVEN YOUR BIN LOOK BEAUTIFUL!

Every child wishes for a snow day, and festive films about white Christmases are always the best ones. This sweater design, with its LED lights, is a visual representation of just how excited I get when I hear the word "snow!" My eyes literally light up. And let's face it: a Christmas sweater book wouldn't be complete without at least one light-up project. An open-weave garment isn't essential here, as LED bulbs are generally small enough to push through most knitted fabrics, but it is important to find an open-weave braid or ribbon for the front as these can often be stiffer. You will find a selection in any good haberdashery. The color of the sweater is up to you, but a vibrant shade contrasts better with the lights.

Materials ✂

- Decorative braid or lacy ribbon
- Needle and coordinating thread
- Scissors
- Set of battery-powered LED lights
- Old sock or fabric pocket-style phone case
- Rubber bands

Method

1. Lay your sweater on a flat surface and arrange your decorative braid or ribbon on the front to spell out the word "SNOW" (or whatever alternative word you have chosen to depict).

2. Sew the braid to the sweater using a straight running stitch (see glossary, page 109) and coordinating thread.

3. Once you have stitched down the lettering, it is time to work out the placement of the LED lights. You may find it easier to get a sense of the finished result if you switch the lights on first.

4. Push the bulbs through one by one from the inside of the sweater, pushing through the fabric and then through a gap in the decorative braid.

5. To ensure the lights stay in place, wrap a rubber band tightly at the back of each light. This helps them grip the fabric and remain in position.

6. The placement of the lights will determine the best spot to sew in your battery pack. This can be popped inside an old baby sock or a fabric phone case and secured to the inside of your sweater. Don't add the battery pack yet, but attach the pouch in position by sewing through the yarn on the inside of the fabric, rather than through to the front, so that the stitches are invisible on the outside of the sweater. Make sure it's attached securely enough to take the weight of the battery pack.

7 Pop the battery pack into the pouch.

8 Take care when putting on or removing this sweater, so that you don't dislodge or pull out the lights.

9 Flick the switch and watch yourself light up!

 *Tip*

Never leave batteries in electrical items for too long as they can leak. Remember to remove them before you pack the sweater away at the end of the season. If you want to wash this sweater, you should remove the rubber bands and lights before doing so.

Baby, It's Cold Outside

WOULDN'T IT BE SAD TO SPEND TIME MAKING THE PERFECT CHRISTMAS SWEATER, AND THEN ONLY GET TO WEAR IT ONCE?

Covered in cute little bobble hats, this winter-themed sweater solves that problem—it looks as good in November or January as it does in December. For anyone itching to get those knitting needles out, here's your opportunity. It's the sole knitting project in the book, so if you're not keen, there are 19 others to choose from! However, these hats are simple enough for an absolute beginner, not to mention tiny and transportable, so you can make them just about anywhere: on the train, in a waiting room or on your sofa. The number of hats you knit is up to you—it's a great way to use up odds and ends of leftover yarn. You can use almost any type of sweater for this project, but avoid very lightweight fabrics as the hats may pull or distort the shape.

Materials

- Size 4 knitting needles
- Selection of double-knit or Aran-weight yarn
- Yarn needle
- Scissors
- Sturdy cardboard
- Pencil and ruler
- Needle and coordinating thread (optional)

Method

1. Cast on 18 stitches. For instructions on "Casting On," see the glossary section, pages 106–7.

2. To create the ribbing for the bottom of the hat, you need to alternately "knit" and "purl" stitches (see pages 107 and 108) to the end of the row (K1, P1). Then switch hands so that the needle with the knitting is back in your left hand and repeat. You need to complete three ribbing rows.

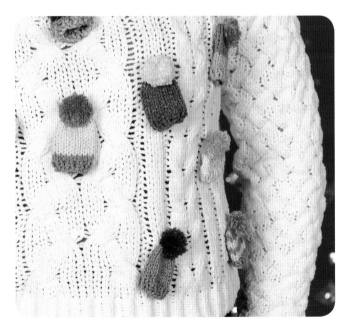

3. Once the ribbing is complete, knit one whole row and then purl the next, repeating until you've created six rows, and then finishing with a final (seventh) row in knit stitch. This is "stockinette stitch" (see glossary, page 108).

4. Once you've completed all the rows, cut the yarn from the ball, leaving a length that is long enough to use for stitching your hat together (approximately 8 inches).

5. Thread your trailing length of yarn onto a yarn needle and pass the needle through each of the stitches left on the knitting needle, picking each one up with the yarn needle and removing it from the knitting needle. Once all the stitches are transferred, pull them into a gather. This is the top of the hat.

6. Using the same length of yarn, join the sides of the hat together with "mattress stitch" (see glossary, page 108).

7. To make a pompom for the top of the hat, use the "Basic Pompom" method shown on page 110 of the glossary section. Use a 2-inch piece of card for this particular project.

 8 When your pompom is ready, thread one of its tails onto the yarn needle, feed it through the center of the hat and complete a few stitches to secure. Knot and trim on the inside of the hat.

9 Repeat steps 1–8 for all your hats and pompoms.

10 Experiment with the placement of the hats before you stitch them to the sweater. You could let the shape of the garment inform the design—for example, if your sweater has a V-neck, you might wish to accentuate it by echoing the "V" shape with hats.

11 Use the second tail from each pompom to attach the mini bobble hats to the sweater. Thread the tail onto the yarn needle, stitch a few times through the fabric of the sweater and tie off on the inside. You may also want to add a couple of small stitches near the bottom of each hat (using needle and thread) to prevent them from flapping or twisting around.

  *Tip*

To make more colorful hats in mixed shades, or to use up scraps of yarn, you can switch to a different colored yarn at any point in either a knit or purl row. Instructions on "Changing Color" are given on page 107. If you have changed color, weave any loose ends into the back of the knitting using a yarn needle before trimming them.

Merry and Bright

ARE YOU A COLLECTOR OF ALL THINGS SPARKLY? IF THE ANSWER'S YES, YOU'LL LOVE THE GENIUS INVENTION THAT IS SEQUIN RIBBON!

Sequin ribbon consists of a row of sequins that come already sewn together along the back, enabling you to lay them down with ease and avoid the painstaking process of attaching them one by one. Flexible and easy to shape, it's the ideal sparkly solution for spelling out words. This project is so versatile and will work on any type of sweater, sweatshirt, or even a poncho if that is your style. If you don't feel merry and bright, choose your own words, if you're customizing a cute cropped sweater or a child-sized garment, you can change the message to fit. When the light hits the sequins, you will look and feel amazing.

Materials

- Sequin ribbon (color of choice)
- Fabric glue
- Scissors
- Needle and coordinating thread

Method

1. Begin by plotting out the sequin ribbon on your sweater to get an idea of letter sizes.

2. Working in stages, use fabric glue to "paint" the first letter on. Gently press the back of the sequin ribbon onto the glue, following the shape of the letter. Continue to place glue, followed by ribbon, until you reach a natural break in the lettering. (For example, the sweater in the photograph has a natural break at the end of the first "r" in "Merry.") Cut the ribbon at this point, but leave it longer than it needs to be, so that you can come back later to secure the end.

3. When you've reached a natural break, go back and add glue above or below the first line of sequins, then lay down a second line of ribbon immediately alongside the first, so that you have a double width. (Although you can buy wider sequin ribbon, it does not offer the same flexibility, so it's better to use two rows of narrower ribbon as described.)

4. Continue this method until you have finished spelling out your chosen message.

 If you want even more sparkle, you can add strips of sequin ribbon to any ribbing on the sleeves or hem, or to any other distinctive features of your sweater. Let your particular garment inform your design!

 Once the glue has dried, it's time to secure the ends of the sequin ribbon with small stitches and then cut off any excess. It is also advisable to secure the ribbon at various points along its length to ensure that the design can be washed without disintegrating.

Fox in the Snow

THERE IS SOMETHING INHERENTLY FESTIVE AND NOSTALGIC ABOUT WINTRY TALES OF WOODLAND CREATURES.

Inspired by the many children's books and Christmas cards that depict foxes running through snow or searching for food under a frozen sky, this pretty design can be customized to your liking in various ways: by changing the size of the fox, using different colors or fabrics, or even creating a different type of woodland animal. The faux-fur tail adds a cosy and tactile twist.

Embellish with as many stars as you like—and if your sweater has a pocket, collar, or other distinguishing feature, you can position your stars to make it into more of a feature. Any type of sweater works for this project.

Materials

- Paper "fox" templates (see page 95)
- Scissors
- Fabric marker pen
- Fleece fabric in color/pattern of choice
- Faux fur
- White felt
- Needle and embroidery floss, two-thread thickness, in coordinating shade
- Dress pins
- Filling/stuffing for tail
- 1 x pearl or bead (optional)
- 2 x black buttons, for eyes
- 1 x large red button, for nose

Method

1. Enlarge the "fox" templates on page 95 using a photocopier. Cut the templates out.

2. Draw around the templates in fabric marker onto your chosen materials and cut out the shapes. You need: 1 x body in fleece, 1 x tail in fleece, 1 x tail in faux fur, 2 x inner-ear shapes in white felt, 5 x stars in white felt, and 1 x moon in white felt.

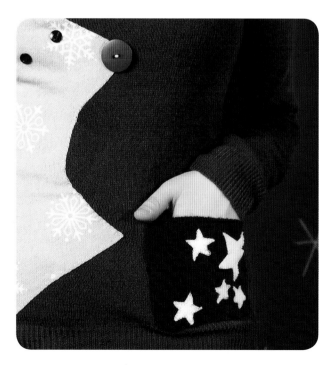

3. Start by attaching the felt inner-ear shapes to the fleece fox's body using embroidery floss and blanket stitch (see glossary, page 99). The sweater in the photograph was stitched using a pale-blue floss, but you might prefer a contrasting shade.

4. Work out the placement of your fox, then pin him to the sweater. Attach using blanket stitch again. (Or you can sew this on a machine, if you have one, for speed.)

5. Place the two tail shapes (in faux-fur and fleece) together, with their "right" sides facing in towards each other. Sew them together around the edges using backstitch (see glossary, page 98), making sure to leave a gap of at least 1 ⅛ inches at one end so you can turn the tail back the right way around. Again use a machine if you prefer.

6 The tail is currently "inside out:" turn it the right way around by easing the fabric out through the hole in the stitching. Stuff the tail to your desired thickness using leftover yarn trimmings, spare pillow filling, or some old tights, anything really as long as the filling is washable. You can buy purpose-made stuffing from some craft shops.

7 Close up the stuffed tail by hand using blind mattress stitch (see glossary, page 108).

8 Attach the tail to your fox at both ends, taking the thread through the fleece backing rather than the faux fur and making sure to pass through the sweater fabric so that it's well secured. If the tail is too heavy to lie flat, add additional stitches where necessary to help keep it in position and prevent it drooping forwards.

9 Use embroidery floss to attach a pearl or bead of your choice to the back of the moon, leaving it on a length so that it dangles in the center and adds a touch of "bling." Felt is a thick, dense fabric so you can secure the pearl/

bead without pushing the thread all the way to the front of the moon; this way the stitch remains hidden. Once the bead is secure, attach the moon to the sweater using blanket stitch.

10 Now add your felt stars to your sweater in your preferred spot. I added mine to the pocket of the sweater to make it into a feature, but yours can go anywhere you like, or you can omit them. Sew in blanket stitch or simply with a straight running stitch in white thread if you prefer (for both techniques, see glossary, page 108).

11 Finally, sew on two black buttons for eyes and a large red button for the fox's festive nose.

Kiss Me

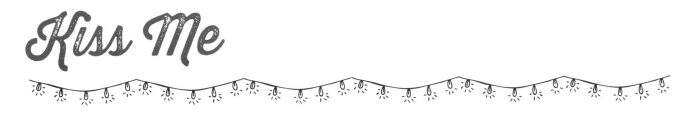

WEARING THIS SWEATER WILL ENSURE YOU GET LUCKY AT THE CHRISTMAS PARTY. . . .
PUT IT ON AND PUCKER UP!

The custom of kissing under the mistletoe has been around since the late 1700s, and it's sometimes said to be bad luck if you find yourself beneath a sprig and then refuse to accept a kiss. Adorned with faux, long-lasting mistletoe, crafted from felt and mini pompoms, this sweater couldn't be easier (or cuter!) to put together and will guarantee you're always in the right place at the right time. You can add as many mistletoe leaves as you like, to increase your chances of success.

Materials

- Paper "mistletoe" templates (see page 97)
- Scissors
- Fabric marker pen
- Green felt
- Fabric glue (optional)
- Needle and coordinating threads
- White felt balls/mini pompoms
- Fine ribbon or pre-made bow (color of choice)

Method

1. Trace the "mistletoe" templates on page 97, or enlarge to the desired size using a photocopier. Cut them out.

2. Draw around the paper templates onto green felt with fabric marker, to create as many mistletoe leaves as you like. Cut out the leaves from the felt.

3. Arrange a bunch of leaves on your sweater, making sure any ink left from the outline is facing down. Secure the leaves in place with fabric glue or a straight running stitch (see glossary, page 109).

4. The white felt balls will resemble the mistletoe "berries:" play around with their placement and once you are happy with their positions, stitch them down securely using white thread. Knot and trim the threads on the inside of the sweater.

5. For a final decorative flourish, tie a small bow from the fine ribbon and sew this securely in place over the uppermost stem of mistletoe.

6. Apply some lipstick and you're ready for a kiss!

Don't Get Cross

IT'S THAT TIME OF MERRIMENT, CHEER, AND FAMILY ARGUMENTS! THIS YEAR, INSTEAD OF CROSS WORDS, FOCUS YOUR ENERGY ON CROSS-STITCH!

It's a running joke that most families fall out at Christmas. Much as we try for best behavior, promising not to bring up old disputes and forcing ourselves to smile politely at the dry brussel sprouts and lumpy gravy, sometimes it's a step too far when we don't get a single item from our carefully considered Christmas list! But this cheery sweater is sure to put everyone in a good mood and will have you feeling very pleased with yourself. For non-crafters it might be the first time you've encountered "aida," the fabric traditionally used for cross stitch, though it's possible you've seen it before, probably on the wall of your granny's house. The fabric comes perforated with a grid of small holes, making it very easy to stitch perfect crosses.

Materials

- Dissolvable aida (for Method 1)
- Masking tape
- Embroidery needle
- Green embroidery floss or fine yarn
- Holly cross-stitch pattern (see page 104)
- Scissors
- Small red felt balls/mini pompoms
- Needle and red thread
- Dressmaker's carbon paper (for Method 3)
- Soft pencil (for Method 3)

Method One – Aida

Dissolvable aida is needed for this project and can be bought easily online or in large craft stores. If you can't find it, there are two alternative methods given for transferring your cross-stitch designs onto your sweater, though Method 1 gives the crispest finish. A garment with a close, flat weave works best here, or even a sweatshirt.

1. Place a piece of dissolvable aida onto your sweater in the spot where you want to stitch your first holly leaf design (see page 87). Hold it in place with masking tape. (If you want to stitch lots of small holly motifs, you can cut the aida down to size before you start.)

2. The aida has the holes arranged on a grid so you can size up your crosses simply by counting the number of holes you choose to have in your square.

3. Use embroidery floss to cross-stitch your motif (see page 87 for the holly pattern and page 104 for the cross-stitch technique). The stitches go through the holes in the aida and the fabric of the sweater. Knot and trim the threads on the inside of the sweater.

4. Remove the masking tape and trim off excess aida from around the edges of the finished design.

5. Repeat for the rest of your holly motifs.

6. Following the directions on the packet, soak the aida in water until fully dissolved. Ta-da! You will be left with only the cross-stitch pattern on your sweater.

7. Using red thread, attach the red balls or pompoms to the leaves to resemble holly berries.

Method Two – Paper

1. Photocopy the holly cross-stitch pattern from page 87, enlarging it to your desired size. Trim off excess paper. Repeat for the desired number of holly motifs.

2. Decide where you want your first holly sprig and use masking tape to hold the pattern in place on the front of the sweater.

3. Carefully stitch though the paper and sweater, positioning your crosses according to the pattern. (See page 104 for the technique.)

4. Repeat for the rest of your holly motifs.

5. When you have finished, soak the paper and remove carefully with a pair of tweezers. This can be a little laborious, so you may need some mulled wine on hand to get you through.

6. Using red thread, attach the red balls or pompoms to the leaves to resemble holly berries.

Method Three – Carbon Paper

1. Photocopy the holly cross-stitch pattern from page 87, enlarging it to your desired size.

2. Place your sweater on a flat surface, lay a sheet of dressmaker's carbon paper onto the fabric, and then position the pattern on top, in the spot where you want your first holly motif.

3. Using a soft pencil, trace over all the crosses in the design. This will transfer a faint chalk impression onto the sweater.

4. Remove the pattern and carbon paper, and stitch over the chalk impression. (See page 104 for the technique.)

5. Repeat for the rest of your holly motifs. Any remaining visible chalk can be rubbed off or washed off once your design is complete.

6. Using red thread, attach the red balls or pompoms to the leaves to resemble holly berries.

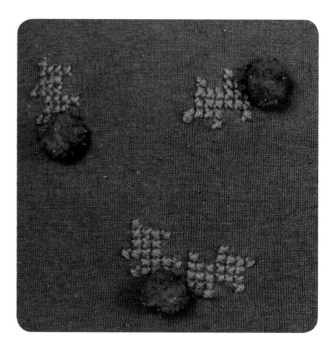

Jingle All the Way

THE FESTIVE SEASON BRINGS COUNTLESS EXCUSES TO BE MERRY AND DANCE. EVEN YOUR GRANNY WILL BE UP AND MOVING TO A CHRISTMAS HIT.

And this sweater is perfect for dancing because when you move, it jingles. And jingles. And jingles! While you may not be stealthy in this sweater, you certainly won't be ignored. The number of bells you choose to add is completely up to you, but I say the more the better. The bells sold by craft shops are generally very light so you can use most types of sweater for this project.

Materials

- Several sheets of paper
- Selection of bells (small, large, gold, silver, etc.)
- Needle and coordinating threads
- Scissors

Method

1. Lay your sweater on a flat, elevated surface. All the bells will be sewed into place on this surface, so avoid doing this project on the floor or your back will suffer!

2. Place sheets of paper inside the sweater so that when you begin to sew your bells into position you don't accidentally sew the front and back of the sweater together.

3. Grab a handful of bells and drop them onto your sweater. If needed, swirl a little with your hand, but at all costs avoid picking up individual bells and forming an organized pattern.

5. Once your bells are in place, stitch them down. There should be a metal loop at the base of each bell. Bring your needle and thread though the front of the sweater from the inside and then through the loop on the bell. Take the needle back through the front of the sweater. Repeat three or four times to secure the bell before tying off the thread inside the sweater.

6. When all the bells are secured, your sweater is ready to wear! Put on your favorite Christmas track and dance around the house to hear just how festive you sound. Jingle jingle!

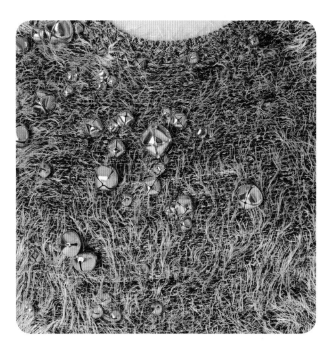

You Better Bow-lieve It

WHAT FASTER WAY TO MAKE THINGS FESTIVE THAN WITH THE SIMPLE APPLICATION OF A BOW?

Come December, my house gets wrapped up in ribbon, with swathes of the stuff spiralled around banisters, festooned over mirrors, draped along the back of chairs and even tied around the stems of potted plants. Each finished off with a beautiful bow, of course. This project enables you to give a sweater the Christmas treatment extremely quickly, even if you're not an avid crafter. You can be as subtle or extravagant as you like, and those who can't resist a bit of sparkle can intersperse their bows with crystals, sequins, or beads. It's probably the fastest project in the book, and if you want to speed it up even more you can buy pre-made bows from most craft stores, although your choice of colors and fabrics will be more restricted than if you create your own from lengths of ribbon.

Materials

- Reel of ribbon (color and type of your choice)
- Sequins or crystal beads (optional)
- Needle and coordinating thread
- Scissors

Method

1 Cut lengths of ribbon and tie them into small bows. You need at least 10–12 or as many as you wish to add to your sweater.

2 Once you have tied your desired number of bows, lay the sweater out on a flat surface and determine the placement of the bows on the sweater.

3 Get all your bows into position before you begin to stitch them down. If you are working on the front and back of the sweater you will have to do this process in two halves.

4 When you are happy with the positioning, bring a threaded needle from the inside of the sweater and out through both the fabric and the center of the bow. Take the needle back through the layers to complete a small stitch. Go over the same stitch four or five times to secure it, then tie off at the back and trim. Repeat for all bows.

5 If you wish to add additional sequins and/ or beads, these normally come with holes for you to stitch through. Sew them on securely, knotting and trimming the threads on the inside of the sweater.

The First Noel

WHY SAY IT IN ENGLISH, WHEN IT FEELS FAR MORE CHIC TO SAY IT IN FRENCH!?

And since Noel is a significantly shorter word than Christmas, not only does it look more sophisticated but it also fits much more comfortably on the front of a sweater. This very simple project is perfect if you need a festive garment fast. It makes use of simple scraps of decorations you might already have around the house or can find in most shops, and since it is easy to dismantle afterwards, you could even customize a sweater that's already in your wardrobe if you don't wish to buy a new one. For an outfit that's more than just temporary, employ the same method but choose embellishments that can be washed.

Materials

- Lengths of wrapping tinsel, tree beads, ribbon, decorative trim, etc.
- Needle and coordinating threads

Method

① Lay your sweater flat on a work surface.

② Experiment with the lengths of your chosen embellishments, positioning them on the front of the sweater to spell out "Noel" or the particular word you have chosen.

③ Once you are happy with the arrangement, secure the lettering using your needle and matching threads to sew a couching stitch (see glossary, pages 102–3). Knot and trim the threads on the inside of the sweater.

④ Prepare to look festively chic!

TEMPLATES AND GLOSSARY

"WE ALL WANT SOME FIGGY PUDDING" (HOLLY CROWN),
PAGE 19

HOLLY LEAF

"DO YOU WANT TO BUILD A SNOWMAN?," PAGE 24

SNOWMAN ARMS

REINDEER ANTLER

REINDEER TAIL

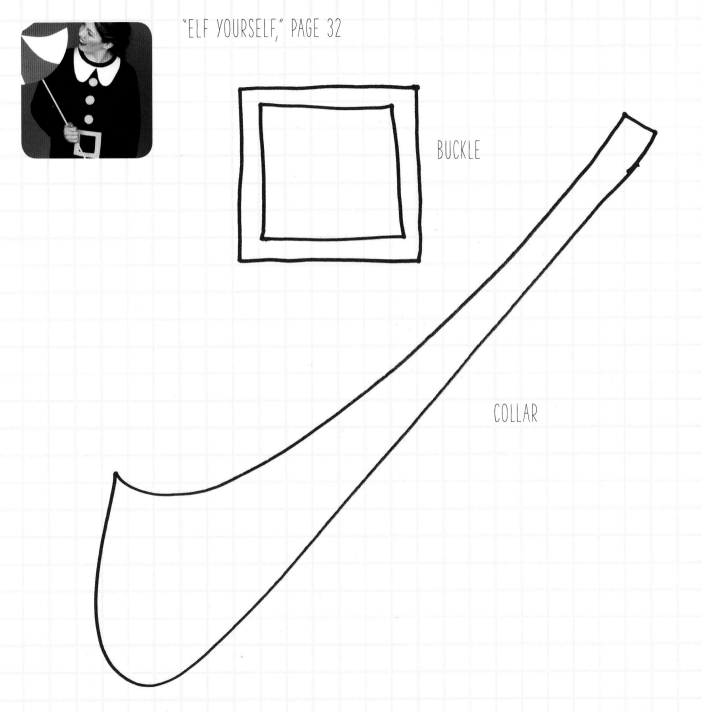

"ELF YOURSELF," PAGE 32

BUCKLE

COLLAR

89

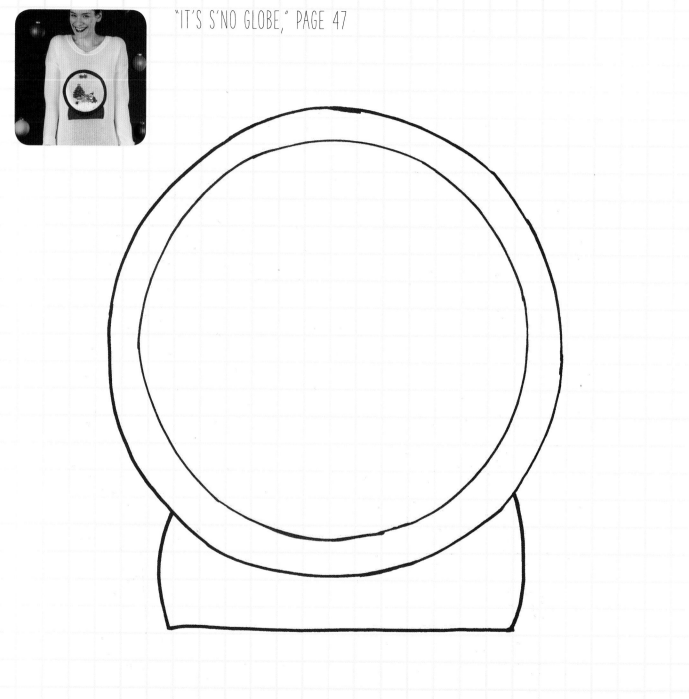

REINDEER

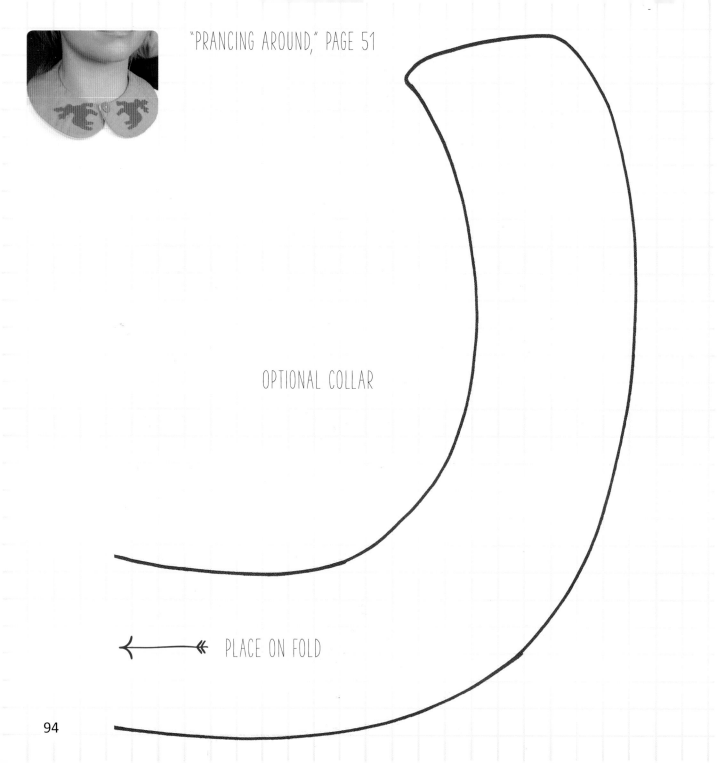

OPTIONAL COLLAR

← ≪ PLACE ON FOLD

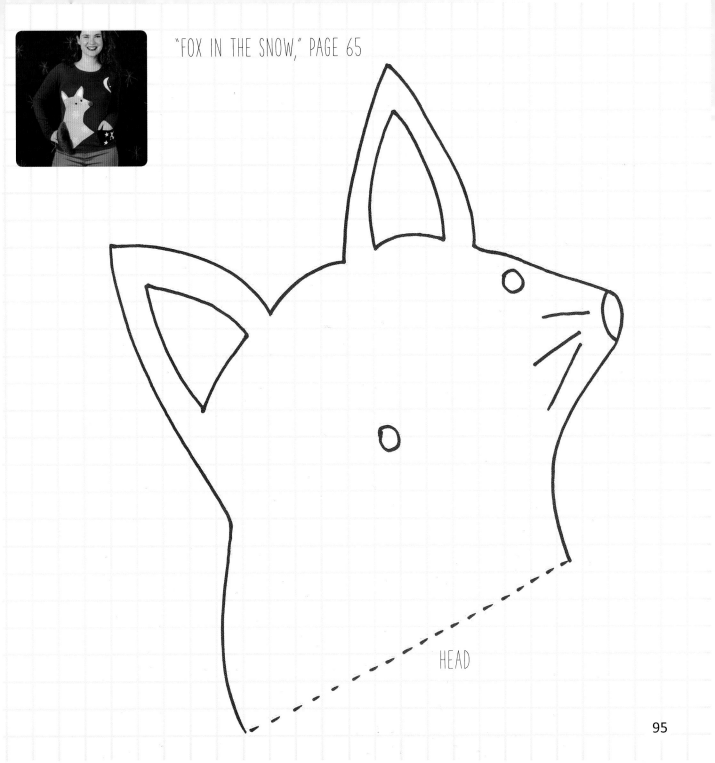

"FOX IN THE SNOW," PAGE 65

HEAD

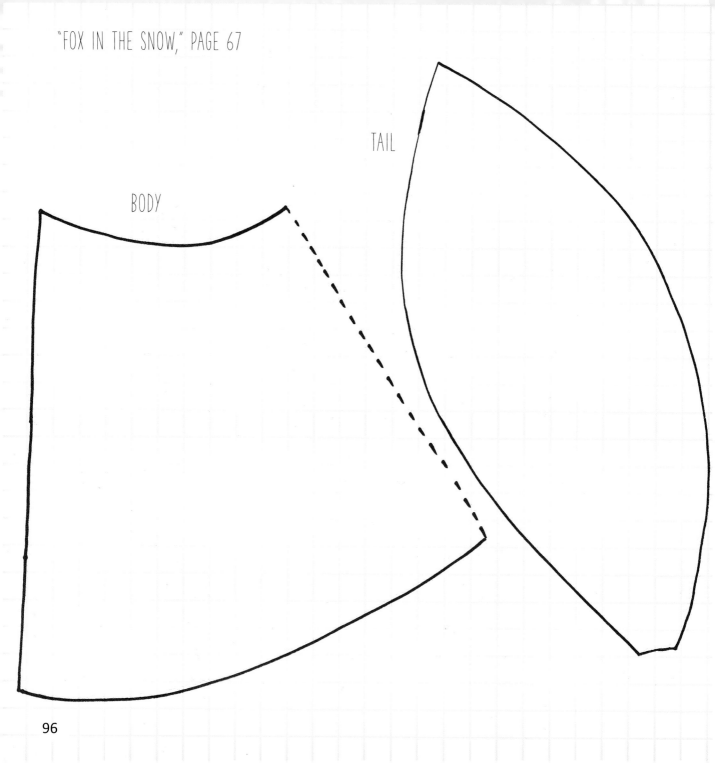

TAIL

BODY

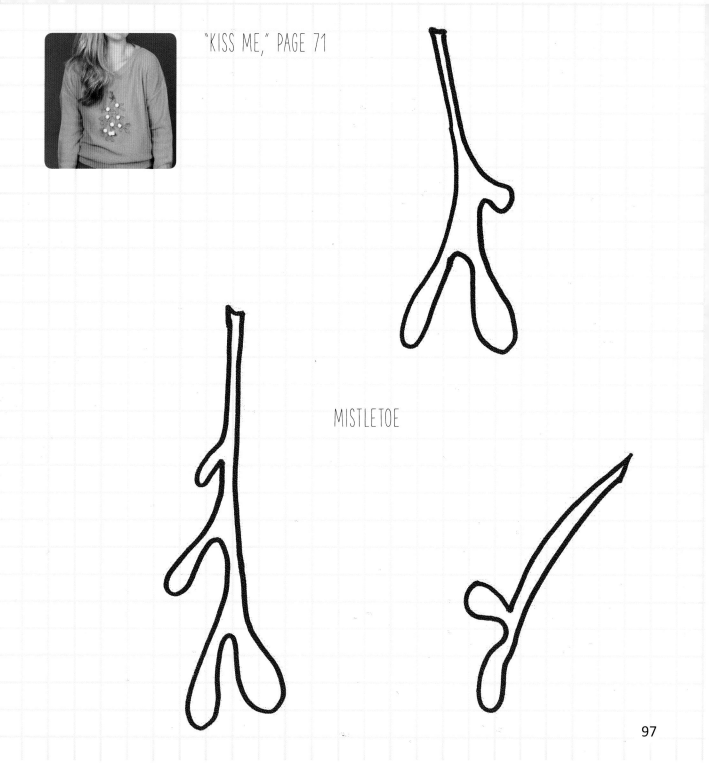

MISTLETOE

GLOSSARY OF SKILLS

This book caters to all skill levels, so even if you're a complete novice, you can still create a fantastic Christmas sweater. This section explains the various stitching and craft techniques used in the book.

BACKSTITCH

This is the most simple hand-sewn stitch that is closest to a strong machine stitch. Thread a sharp needle and knot one end of the thread. Bring your needle up from the underneath of the fabric at (1). Push it back through at (2) then up again at (3). When done correctly, the stitches will look quite long at the back and small and neat on the front.

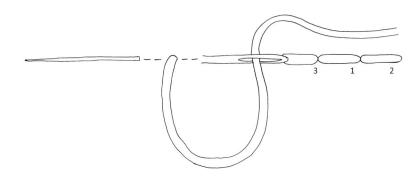

BLANKET STITCH

This is a stitch that can be used to add a decorative element or to close up or reinforce an edge, so it's perfect for appliqué. Working from left to right, the twisted edge forms a continuous line of sewing, connecting up short parallel stitches which go off at right angles. Bring the needle up at (1), down at (2), and up at (3) with the thread looped under the needle. Pull the needle to tighten each stitch individually.

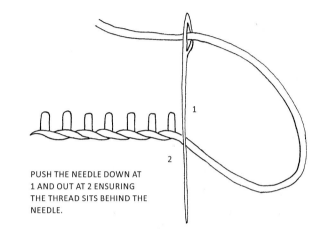

PUSH THE NEEDLE DOWN AT 1 AND OUT AT 2 ENSURING THE THREAD SITS BEHIND THE NEEDLE.

BLIND LADDER STITCH

This stitch is the best way to close up unsightly gaps. For example, when sewing an item like a pillow or pouch, where you want the sewing hidden away on the inside, it's necessary to sew the pieces of fabric together with their "right" sides facing inwards and leave a gap in the sewing so that you can later turn the piece back the right way around. To then close the gap so that it looks just like the rest of the stitching, you use blind ladder stitch (sometimes called slip stitch).

To close the opening, fold under the edges of the fabric so that you have a clean folded edge on both sides of the gap. Thread a sharp needle and knot the end of the thread. Slip the needle and thread under the fold of one of the edges (I start with the edge closest to me but it does not matter which side you begin with). Bring the needle all the way up through the fabric so that the knot is tucked out of sight under the fold. Exactly opposite the place where you pulled the thread up, push the needle point into the top of the opposite fold and back through to the underneath of the fabric. Then move the needle along the underside of the folded edge as though you are making a small stitch. Bring the needle up through the folded fabric again. Pull though and put the needle down in the opposite fold at the corresponding point again. Continue moving the stitches along under the folds. Finish with a tiny double stitch. The join will be invisible, just like the rest of your sewing on this particular item.

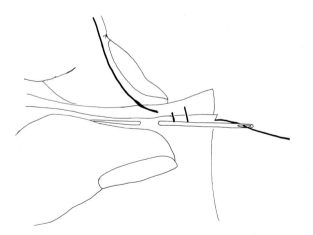

Couching is a wonderfully useful stitch in the world of hand embroidery as it allows you to be truly versatile with the textures and yarns you add to a project. To couch, you need to lay down the ribbon, yarn, beading, or whatever it is that you want to attach, and then stitch over it at intervals.

You have two choices with couching; one is to make the stitches almost invisible, the other is to highlight them and make them a feature of the design. Either way, you do this through the choice of thread, matching or contrasting it to the project, and sizing the stitches small or miniscule.

The first thing you need to do is to deal with the end of the laid thread (i.e. the thing you are couching, which could in fact be anything, such as ribbon, cord, or even tinsel). You may be able to secure the end using a "plunging" method. To do this, push the point of a needle with a large eye into your fabric at the point where you want the end to be, then thread

the ribbon/cord/tinsel through the eye of the needle and pull through. Remove the needle and secure at the back with a few stitches with a sharp needle and thread. If you are couching something that is too thick to be pulled through or fit into the eye of a needle, you can instead tuck the end under itself and secure with your first couching stitch.

To sew a couching stitch, thread a sharp needle with your chosen couching thread (an ordinary sewing thread in a matching or contrasting color to the laid thread). Bring the threaded needle up from the back, next to the point where you want your laid thread to go. Hold the laid thread in place with your thumb, leaving an inch or two on the end, and push the needle down on the opposite side to where you brought it up, trapping the laid thread underneath your stitch. Repeat this at regular intervals. This is basic couching and is a useful skill for adding glitz to your sweater.

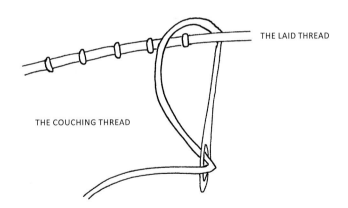

THE LAID THREAD

THE COUCHING THREAD

CROSS-STITCH

To make a line of cross-stitch, begin at the right-hand side of where you want the row to be. You will stitch right to left. Bring the needle up at (1), down at (2). Up at (3) and down at (4), then bring the needle up at (5), down at (3), up at (6) and down at (2). Continue the same pattern along the row.

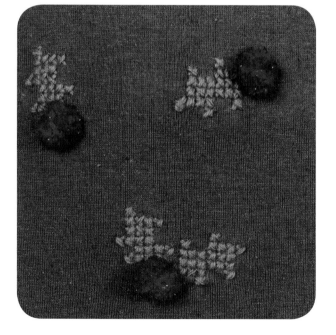

FLY STITCH

This is a very easy stitch to master. The shape you are aiming to create looks like a "Y." You can alter the look of the stitch by varying the length of the base of the Y. Bring the needle up at (1) and down at (2). Bring the needle up in the center of the stitch at (3), trapping the thread of the stitch and then putting your needle back down at (4). You can change the length of this part of the Y by increasing the distance of (4) from the start of the stitch.

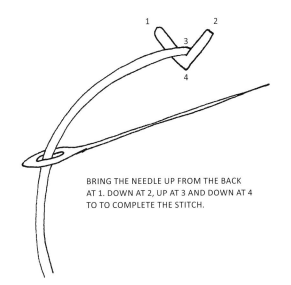

BRING THE NEEDLE UP FROM THE BACK AT 1. DOWN AT 2, UP AT 3 AND DOWN AT 4 TO TO COMPLETE THE STITCH.

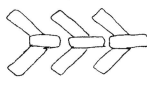

A ROW OF FLY STITCHES

CASTING ON

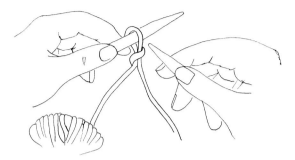

1. PLACE A SLIP KNOT ON THE LEFT NEEDLE

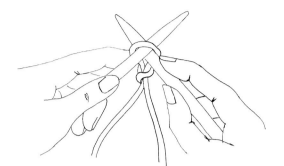

2. PUSH THE TIP OF THE RIGHT NEEDLE THROUGH THE SLIP KNOT SO THAT THE RIGHT NEEDLE IS BEHIND THE LEFT ONE

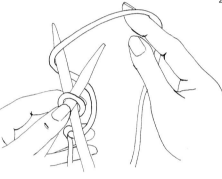

3. WRAP THE WORKING YARN COUNTER-CLOCKWISE AROUND THE RIGHT NEEDLE

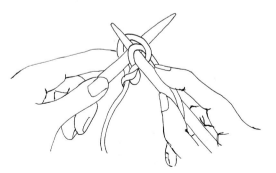

4. MOVE YOUR NEW LOOP GENTLY OFF THE RIGHT NEEDLE AND ONTO THE LEFT ONE

5. REPEAT THE PROCESS IN THE TOP LOOP AND CONTINUE UNTIL YOU HAVE THE NUMBER OF STITCHES YOU REQUIRE ON THE LEFT NEEDLE

KNITTING TECHNIQUES

CASTING ON

Casting on is the term used in knitting to describe the process of adding the first stitches to a needle before you start to knit. There are a number of different methods of casting on. Some give a different edge that is suited to a particular item, such as a stretchy edge for socks, while others are just a matter of preference. The method explained here is called "knitting on" and is perfect for new knitters as it's the simplest technique to learn.

Tie a slip-knot on the left needle (see diagram 1). Keep the ball of yarn behind your needles at all times. Place the right needle into the front of the loop and push the needle through so the tips of the needles cross and the right needle is behind the left one. The yarn you use to knit with is referred to as the "working yarn." Bring the working yarn around the right needle counter-clockwise so that it sits between the crossed needles. Keeping the yarn wrapped on the right needle, pull the tip of the right needle down so that it sits on top of the left needle. Now there will be a loop on the right needle: this is your stitch. Move the needle tips apart and carefully transfer the stitch from the right needle to the left. You now have two stitches on the left needle. Continue this process until you have the correct number of stitches required.

CHANGING YARN COLOR

In knitting, the yarn can be changed at any point, regardless of whether you are creating a knit or purl row, and it can be done at any point in the row. To join a new yarn, place the right knitting needle into the stitch as normal. Instead of wrapping the yarn you have been using, loop the new color around the needle and make the stitch with that yarn, continuing the row with the new color. Gently hold the tail of the new color against the knitting with your finger to keep it in place. Once you have completed a few stitches, there will be no longer be any need to do this, as the yarn will be secure.

KNIT STITCH

Perhaps you're thinking "aren't all knitting stitches 'knit' stitch?" In fact, there are two main stitches used in knitting: one is knit stitch and the other is purl stitch (see page 108). Having already cast on (see page 106), hold the needle with the stitches in your left hand. (If you are left-handed you should still knit this way as it determines the knit pattern.) Insert the tip of the right needle into the first stitch from front to back, the same way you did when casting on. With your right index finger, bring yarn from the working yarn counter-clockwise around the point of the right needle. Unlike casting on, slip the stitch off the needle instead of passing it over to the left needle.

PURL STITCH

Purl stitch is the other main stitch used in knitting, besides knit stitch (see page 107). A purled stitch looks just like the back of your knit stitch, so it is essentially a back-to-front knit stitch. The needle holding all of the stitches will be in your left hand. Place the tip of the right needle into the top of the first stitch so that the right needle remains in front when crossing the left one. Take the working yarn from the ball and wrap it counter-clockwise around and between the needles. Gently push the tip of the right needle up, lifting the stitch off as you did for the knit stitch. Continue to the end of the row.

STOCKINETTE STITCH

This is a basic knitting technique and is the building block for most knitting patterns. It is created by alternating rows of knit stitch (see page 107) and purl stitch (see above) to give a V-patterned look.

MATTRESS STITCH

This stitch is used to join the seams of knitting together. Begin by lining up the seam edges, with the "right" sides of the knitted pieces facing up. Thread a darning needle with the yarn from the tail of one of your ends (it's always best to leave tails long for exactly this reason). Look at the lined-up seam stitches and you will see they resemble small Vs. Move the thread from right to left behind the V-shaped stitches, continuing down until you reach the bottom of the knitted piece. Blind mattress stitch is used to invisibly close gaps in stitched fabric.

This is the cornerstone of all stitching. Thread a needle and knot one end of the thread or yarn. (Always use sharp scissors when cutting lengths of thread or yarn and lick and flatten the end to make it easier to push through the eye of your needle.) Pierce the needle through the "wrong" side of the fabric and pull through until it stops at the knot. On a loose-weave knitted sweater fabric, be careful not to pull too hard or the knot will come though. (After the first few stitches your sewing will be secure and you don't need to worry about accidentally pulling it through).

To make your first stitch, push your needle back into the fabric close to the point at which you came up. How far apart you decide to do this determines the length of your stitch, so if you want small stitches leave only a small gap. Pull the thread back through to the wrong side. You have just made your first stitch—it felt good, didn't it? The stitch should lie flat without bunching the fabric.

Once you become confident, you can sew more than one stitch at a time. To do this, bring the point of your needle up from the back, (needle only, not the thread as well), then put the needle back through the fabric, still without pulling the thread through. Repeat this as many times as you can (probably about four stitches in one go) until you run out of room on the needle. The final time you bring the needle up, also pull the thread through and it will now follow the same journey the needle made, running through each of the holes and producing four stitches (or however many you made). When using this method, be careful not to let tangles form at the back of your work.

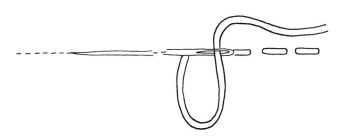

POMPOMS

You can make all of the pompoms needed in this book, both large and tiny, using this method. Cut a rectangular piece of card approximately half the diameter of the desired size of your finished pompom. Begin wrapping your chosen yarn around the center of the card and continue doing so until it is nice and thick. Slide the wrapped yarn off the card and tie tightly through the center with a second piece of matching yarn. You will be left with a loop of yarn nipped in at the middle. Cut through the tops of all the loops and fan out the strands, then give your pompom a haircut to trim down the ends and shape it into a ball. To alter the size of your pompom, experiment with smaller or larger pieces of card.

WRAP YOUR YARN AROUND THE CARD TO MAKE THE POMPOM

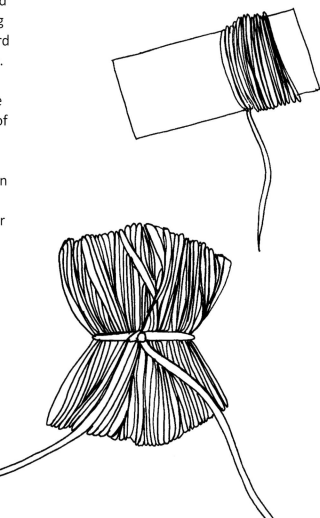

ABOUT THE AUTHOR

Full-time writer, crafter, parent, and vampire-hunter hobbyist, Nicolette Lafonseca established her writing career on her lifestyle blog "Archie and the Rug" where her exuberance and wit shone through, whilst barely masking her contempt for people who spell "a lot" as "alot." Her list of achievements are many and include: kicking cancer in the teeth repeatedly, winning a number of blogging awards, presenting on Channel 4, and giving birth to a fantastic boy. She aspires to rule us all one day with an iron fist . . . of friendship.

Nicolette lives with her family and their excitable hound in a constant flux of refurbishing and decorating in Hebden Bridge in the weather-smattered county of Yorkshire.

www.archieandtherug.com

ACKNOWLEDGMENTS

As it turns out, books are a lot of hard work and they take more than just the dedication and time of the author, so I would like to take this opportunity to thank a few people that helped this book happen.

First up is my ever-loving, long-suffering husband. Not only has he supported me and encouraged me in my career, but he has lived in a house of tinsel and sequins for two years during the creation of this book. Also, my beautiful, perfect baby boy was very understanding about giving up time with Mummy.

I would like to thank Jane Graham Maw and Jennifer Christie, my agents for taking a chance on me and sticking with their crazy northern client.

I would also like to thank Ione Walder who fought for this book and worked tirelessly with me to make it happen.

A big thank you to Hannah Read-Baldrey and Tiff Mumford (and all the people who appeared in my book) for bringing my designs to life. I would also like to thank the team at Quercus, the unsung heroes, who turn ideas into books and make sure they get onto bookshelves.

Huge thanks to all of my blog readers who helped me get where I am. Every time I see my stats I am happy that I am still creating content you enjoy.

Finally, thank you for buying my book.

Take care and Merry Christmas!

Nicolette x